A NEW LOOK AT BARGELLO

The Florentine Needlepoint Stitch Book

CAROL CHENEY ROME

Crown Publishers, Inc., New York

FOR EMILY

Photography by the Author

© 1973 by Carol Cheney Rome

Library of Congress Catalog Card Number: 72-96643

Printed in the United States of America
Published simultaneously in Canada by
General Publishing Company Limited

Design by Nedda Balter

Acknowledgments

I could not have undertaken this book without the cheerful and patient help of Glen Hannah, who rendered the designs into finished pieces of embroidery. My very special thanks to her. Thanks are also due Larry Salmon, Curator of Textiles at the Museum of Fine Arts, Boston, for his help on the historical section. I am deeply appreciative of Ruth Heller's generosity. Six of her excellent designs are shown here worked into Bargello pieces. And my appreciation to Mary Cooke Woodward, who invented the cover design in a magnificent burst of ingenuity. Thanks to Dick, Martha, Bruce, my friends and students for their inspiration and remarkable forbearance.

CONTENTS

Acknowledgments 3

Introduction 7

Florentine Filler Stitches 14

  1 Brick 15
  2 Gobelin Droit 16
  3 Hungarian 17
  4 Hungarian Ground 18
  5 Parisian 19
  6 Old Florentine 20
  7 Zigzag 21

New-Old Florentine Patterns 22

  8 Shaded Peaks 23
  9 Spools 24
 10 Op Boxes 26
 11 Goal Posts 27
 12 Fish Scales 28
 13 Shell Waves 29
 14 Rickrack 30
 15 Triangle Trees 31
 16 Interlocked Chevrons 32
 17 Tweed 33
 18 Laced Ribbons 34

New-Old Florentine Border Patterns 36

 19 Echo Border 37
 20 Ribbed Stripe Border 38
 21 Sawtooth Border 39
 22 Peasant Border 40

New Florentine Patterns 41

 23 Patchwork Sampler 42
 24 Symmetrical Tartan 43
 25 Asymmetrical Tartan 44
 26 Oriental Medallion 46
 27 Interlocked Frames 49
 28 Fantasy Trees 50

Using Florentine Stitches in Representational Designs

Using Florentine Stitches
in Representational Designs   52

    29 Medieval Horse   54
    20 Circus Elephant   58
    31 Rooster   62
    32 Fish   66

Notes on Design   68

Index   79

These two pillows are contemporary Florentine designs. The large pillow, Oriental Medallion, is a four-way design shown on pages 46–48. The small pillow has a traditional peaked design, and a Florentine border has been added to the edges. A detail of the design is shown on page 70.

Introduction

Bargello is a name that covers a whole family of needlepoint stitches worked on canvas. These stitches reached a high level of development in the late 1500s and have flourished since then. Other names you may have heard that are synonymous with Bargello are Florentine, Hungarian Point (Point d'Hongrie), and flame (fiamma).

There is more legend than fact surrounding the development of this family of stitches, which undoubtedly has given rise to the number of names associated with it. One of the most popular stories tells of a medieval Hungarian princess marrying into the powerful Medici family and bringing with her to Florence a trousseau embroidered with strange and exotic stitching. Hence, the names Hungarian Point and Florentine embroidery.

The name Bargello has been popularized by one writer who places the origins of these stitches in the Bargello, which was once a prison and is now the great museum in Florence. The name "flame" (fiamma in Italian) describes the look of a particular pattern in the family. Most scholars refer to the family as Florentine work, which is the most comprehensive designation. The terms Florentine and Bargello shall be used here interchangeably.

Classical Florentine work is easy to distinguish from other kinds of canvas embroidery, or needlepoint, for two reasons. First, the stitches are worked on the canvas either horizontally or vertically; they do not cross canvas intersections. Second, the stitches are characteristically worked in various patterns of steps and blocks forming repeat geometric designs. In addition to the famous flame patterns, many stylized floral motifs, chevrons, zigzags, and other designs were developed. These have been used extensively to embellish both ecclesiastical pieces and domestic articles. Florentine work has been particularly popular for upholstery.

Traditionally, Bargello patterns were set up in parallel unbroken or broken rows, with the basic outline of the design filled in with subsequent interlocking rows. Usually two or three color groups were used with

This quaint little pocketbook was stitched in New England in the eighteenth century. The design, which is typically Florentine, is made up of an interesting series of jagged lines and geometric shapes in shaded colors. Note the care with which the design has been centered on the piece and the slight variation in pattern due to miscounting. Courtesy, Museum of Fine Arts, Boston, Gift of Mrs. Luke Vincent Lockwood

several intermediate shades in each group. This shading gave great depth and richness to the otherwise simple designs. While the shading effect can be used to great advantage in contemporary pieces, it is not necessary to stay within these bounds when planning a design.

It is also unnecessary to stay within the bounds of the classical repeat geometric patterns when working with Bargello, and there are historical precedents for using the patterns in other ways. Occasionally, Florentine work was used in combination with another kind of embroidery, with the Florentine areas serving as a frame or border to the main design elements. This is an especially effective treatment for finishing off a new piece of work.

In other cases, one or two Florentine stitches were used to carry out a pictorial design. Where you might have expected to see the classical petit point or Tent stitch used, instead you see Bargello. The use of Bargello stitches in a pictorial, or representational, design, then, is not a new idea. However, we seem to have forgotten this technique of enriching our canvas embroideries and have come to consider Bargello an "either-or" proposition. Either you worked a traditional pattern in shaded colors or you set the whole Bargello family aside and used other needlepoint stitches to work the piece.

This bench cover has a contemporary feeling that belies the fact that it was stitched in the 1700s. The design sections are outlined in a dark color, and the sections are shaded within to create a fantastically rich, intricate pattern with great depth and interest. You may notice that there is a substantial amount of inconsistency within the various sections of the design, but this seems to add to rather than detract from the overall look of the piece. Courtesy, Museum of Fine Arts, Boston, Gift of Miss E. A. Clark in memory of Mary Crowninshield

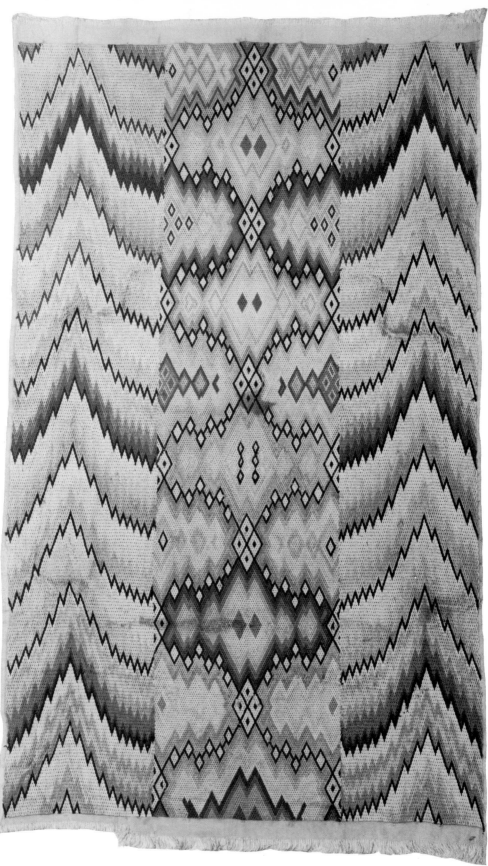

This panel, which was stitched in America in the early 1900s, is a good example of the flame pattern of jagged peaks worked in shaded colors. The piece is made doubly interesting by the inclusion of the center section of diamond shapes and shows how effective more than one Florentine pattern can look when used together. Courtesy, Museum of Fine Arts, Boston, The Elizabeth Day McCormick Collection

This book starts with a section of basic Bargello "filler" stitches that can be used by themselves to cover a whole piece, but which are more effectively used to fill in specific sections of a design. Putting several stitches together makes a piece much more pleasing to work and gives a wonderful textured appearance to the finished embroidery.

Following the section on filler stitches is a section of updated Florentine patterns and a selection of border designs. Then, some patterns are shown that take a new approach to the Florentine idea, including two tartans and three kaleidoscopic, or "four-way," designs.

The collection of designs is concluded with a group of four animals, in which the pictorial Bargello design idea is revived and brought up to date. These designs demonstrate the use of the filler stitches.

Some instruction on planning your own Bargello pieces comes at the end. Watch for the hints in boxes as you go along to help make your Florentine needlepoint experience a fruitful and enjoyable one.

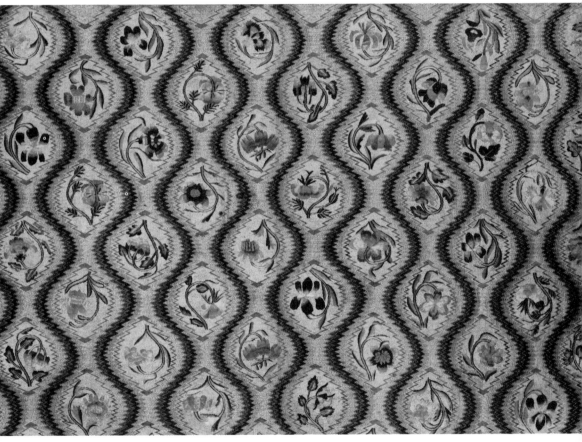

This beautiful Italian altar frontal was worked in the seventeenth century in silk threads on linen. As you can see, two different techniques were used. The flowers were worked in extremely fine split-stitch embroidery, and they were framed with a larger-gauge Florentine pattern of "serrated" wavy lines. There is a feeling of great movement within the piece, almost of swirling, from the Florentine framing and the highly curved lines of the flowers. It is impossible to imagine how long it took to complete this piece; its dimensions are 3' × 6'! Courtesy, Museum of Fine Arts, Boston, The Elizabeth Day McCormick Collection

This piece was made to cover a chair seat. It was stitched in Italy in the seventeenth or eighteenth century in silk thread on linen. The stylized floral design is worked in a Florentine stitch resembling Brick in two directions, and the background is a Zigzag pattern which can be found later in the book on page 21. Some outlining has been done in certain areas of the design to strengthen the shapes and to make them stand out from the background. Courtesy, Museum of Fine Arts, Boston, The Elizabeth Day McCormick Collection

This Florentine altar frontal was worked in Italy, most likely in the seventeenth century, in silk thread on linen. The whole picture is worked in a Brick-type stitch. Notice how the design is made to fill up most of the space; there is very little background area. The little internal border of modified diamond shapes is an effective way to separate the two main design areas. Courtesy, Museum of Fine Arts, Boston, The Elizabeth Day McCormick Collection

Florentine Filler Stitches

The seven stitches that follow are designated as Florentine filler stitches and, used in various combinations, form the classical Florentine patterns developed during past decades. These are the basic units or elements, and it is highly recommended that you work a sampler of these stitches if you are not familiar with them.

Keep the filler stitches in mind when it comes time to work the background of a new piece of needlepoint. They are quick to work up and add texture to your piece. Or, use the stitches within the design itself. Later in the book, you will see examples of the filler stitches used in combination to form abstract and representational designs.

Hem the edges of your canvas with masking tape to prevent them from raveling.

Brick

Brick is probably the most basic Florentine stitch. Various patterns of peaks, scallops, and chevrons are made by setting up parallel rows of Brick outlining the design, and then filling in with different colors. The stitch is usually worked over two or four canvas threads, skipping two vertical threads in between each stitch. The rows interlock, forming the characteristic brickwork pattern. It should be noted that the stitch does not work out over an odd number of canvas threads, such as three or five.

In the variations shown here, you can see the cobbled effect that doubling the stitch can create. This immensely useful stitch is easy to work. The 2-count version is extremely tight and handy to use in small detailed areas. Over a 4-count, Brick moves along quickly and makes a strong, textured background.

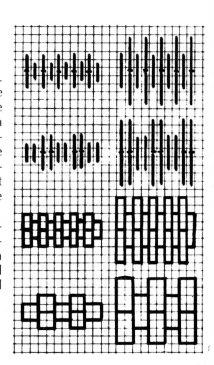

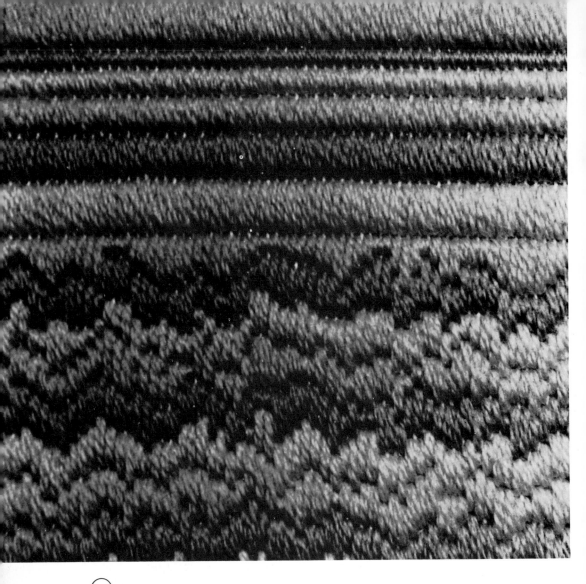

2

Gobelin Droit

This stitch is a very old one, first made to imitate tapestry. At the top of the photograph, the stitch is shown worked in even rows. This is useful for outlining and creating ridges where distinct lines between rows will not be a distraction. The one problem this stitch sometimes creates as a filler stitch is that it allows canvas to show through between rows. This unattractive element can be corrected by painting the canvas beneath in a matching color or by backstitching between the rows to cover the canvas. Backstitching can be done in a matching color or in a contrasting one to create a special design effect. When working Gobelin Droit, stitch with an easy but firm tension; keep the stitches firm and plump.

At the bottom of the photograph, Gobelin Droit is shown worked over an uneven count. Here, straight stitches are worked "freehand" over varying numbers of horizontal threads. This variation is very useful for making interesting terrain and backgrounds.

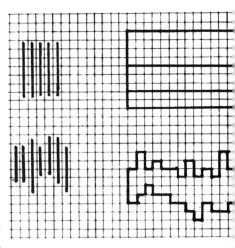

3

Hungarian

This very popular stitch is as useful as it is old. Done over the small count (shown in the upper left of the photograph and diagram), the stitch creates tiny diamond shapes that add a great deal of texture to any design. You can see how the same stitch looks worked in two colors in the upper right portion of the photograph. At the bottom, Hungarian is shown worked over a larger count, and the diamond pattern becomes more dominant. You can create a harlequin effect by working the large-count Hungarian diamonds in different, highly contrasting colors.

When working the stitch, remember to skip two vertical threads in between diamond units or the pattern will not lock together correctly.

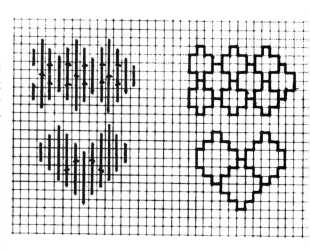

4

Hungarian Ground

In Hungarian Ground, a row of zig-zags is added between the diamond units. The stitch is shown here over a small and a large count to give you an idea of its versatility. There are a number of options to consider concerning color. The zigzag rows can all be one color with the diamonds worked in one or several colors. Or, you can work the zigzag rows in different colors for even greater contrast.

This is an especially fine background stitch and is strong enough to be used by itself to cover an entire piece without appearing monotonous. The stitch works up very quickly if you set up several zigzag rows first and then fill in the diamonds.

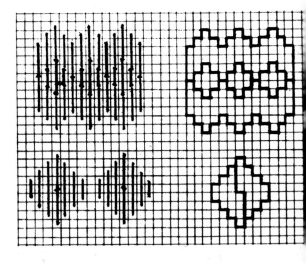

5

Parisian

Parisian is a good texture stitch and can be used in fairly small design areas. Note how different the appearance is when the stitch is worked in two colors. The two-color version looks almost like polka dots. When working with two colors, fill in a row of long stitches and follow with the short stitches in between. Then go on to the next row.

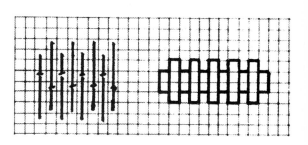

Old Florentine

Old Florentine worked in one color is reminiscent of pavement and makes an excellent background stitch. In two or more colors, the stitch takes on a very festive look and can be used as a design element in itself to cover an entire project. This stitch is quick to work up and is more effective in large areas than in small.

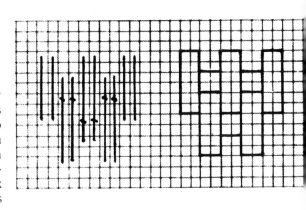

> Stitch a few extra rows around your project to be taken up in the seams during the mounting process, and leave a 1½″ to 2″ blank margin all around for blocking.

7

Zigzag

This lovely stitch can be seen in the heritage piece on page 12, where it is used as a background in a single color. The photograph here shows the stitch worked in one color as well as in two different variations. It is amazing to see what happens to the same stitch depending on the arrangement of colors.

The stitch is actually made up of little triangles that fit together to form the zigzags. You will notice that the stitches are at right angles to the zigzags in contrast to the zigzags in Hungarian Ground, where the stitches are directional with the peaks. When working this stitch, keep a firm tension so no lumps will appear where the triangles come together in the middle of the zigzags.

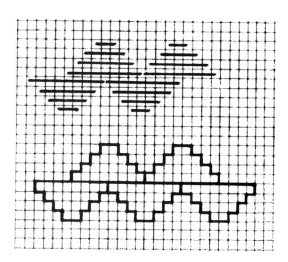

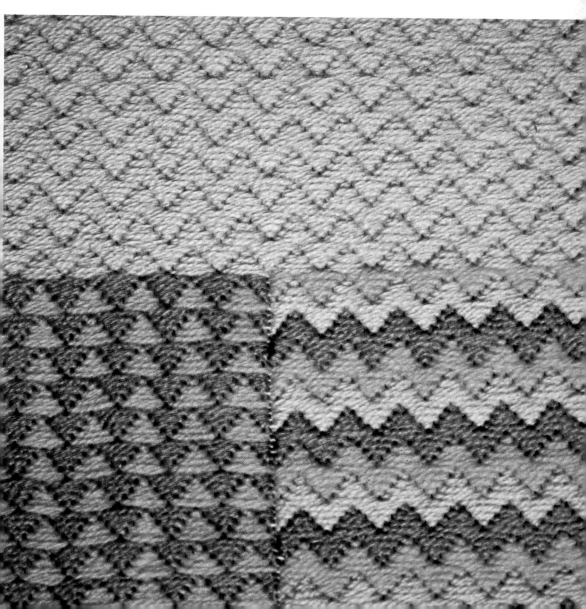

This contemporary pattern, called Rickrack, is based on the Bargello tradition. In this design, bold zigzag lines surround large and small diamonds. This design is shown in color on page 30.

New-Old Florentine Patterns

It becomes a fascinating challenge to create "modern" patterns using the basic principles of Bargello needlepoint. The main rule is to work the stitch units either vertically or horizontally on the canvas; no crossed stitches. You may want to start simply with horizontal rows that lock together and are shaded in the classical tradition, and then move on to more complicated ideas like the cover design, where the stitches are worked in two directions.

It is important to remember to count out the design very carefully as you set it up, or you will find discrepancies in your work that will detract from the finished appearance. Sometimes a counting error will mean that the design won't fit together correctly, and you will have to rip work out. Some designs may have to be centered left-right, top-bottom, or both. Keep this in mind when you start to stitch.

8

Shaded Peaks

This traditional-looking Florentine pattern is set up in horizontal rows. The stitches are worked over six canvas threads (or, are six canvas threads long), moving up or down four to get the steep inclines. Notice that there are groups of three stitches at the tops and bottoms of the peaks and valleys. For variation, you can add or subtract from these groups to get a sharper or more gradual change in the lines. Three shades of the same color family are used here. For another effect, try using unrelated colors.

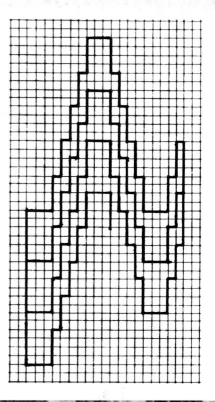

Spools

This is another very simple pattern that depends a great deal on the colors used to create an interesting effect. Here the shades of gold and blue give the piece a mottled, or dappled, look which is reminiscent of undersea photographs. The design is made up of small units worked over eight-six-four-two-two-four-six-eight horizontal canvas threads. You will probably be working with more than one threaded needle at a time, so be careful not to let the threads get snarled.

This pattern worked in one-color rows makes a nice background, as shown in the Fish on pages 66–67.

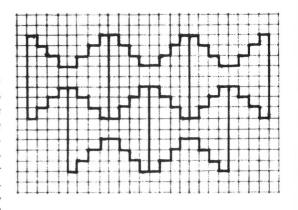

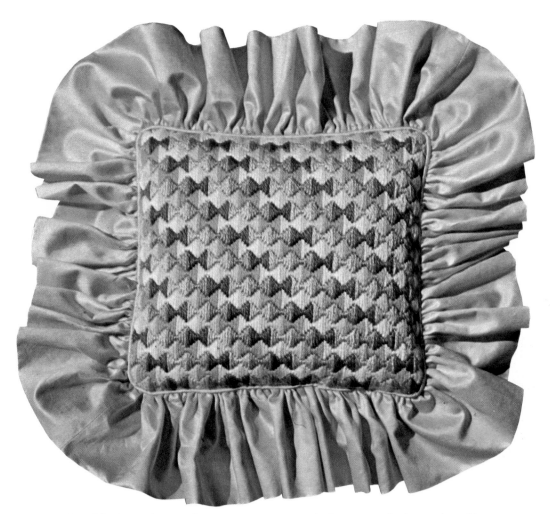

After blocking, the needlepoint piece was made into a small, decorative pillow. The backing fabric is polished cotton, which makes up into a nice ruffle. You can make a small piece look larger by adding a ruffle or fringe or by using the needlepoint as an insert in the center of a larger pillow or background.

Use all colorfast materials in your work. Make a patch test of any "unknown" marking pens or paints you want to use before committing your canvas to them. Use only brand-name yarns guaranteed colorfast.

Op Boxes

This pattern is made up of groups of Gobelin Droit stitches in alternating colors. It is worked over six canvas threads with six stitches in each grouping. This is an excellent example of a pattern that will not work out evenly if you turn the stitches for one color at right angles to the stitches in the other color; this is an occasional frustration you will encounter during Bargello "invention" sprees. Work all the units in the same direction. If you find that the canvas is showing through between rows, work in a backstitch in a matching color.

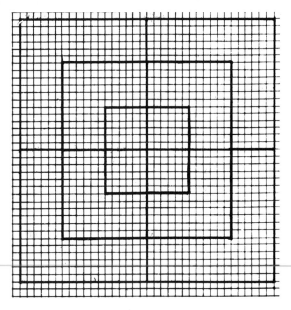

11

Goal Posts

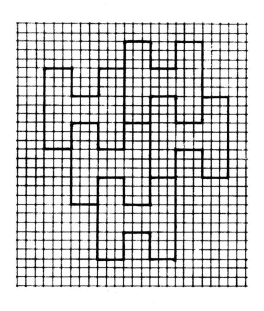

This pattern is made up of H-shaped units; the legs of the H are over nine canvas threads, and the bars are over three. A diagonal row of one color is worked moving over three and up or down six to find the location for the next H.

There are any number of variations that can be worked. You might want to make all the H units on the same plane below or next to each other the same color, and start your patterning from there. Or, you could randomly sprinkle colors throughout the design. Shading the colors will produce yet another effect.

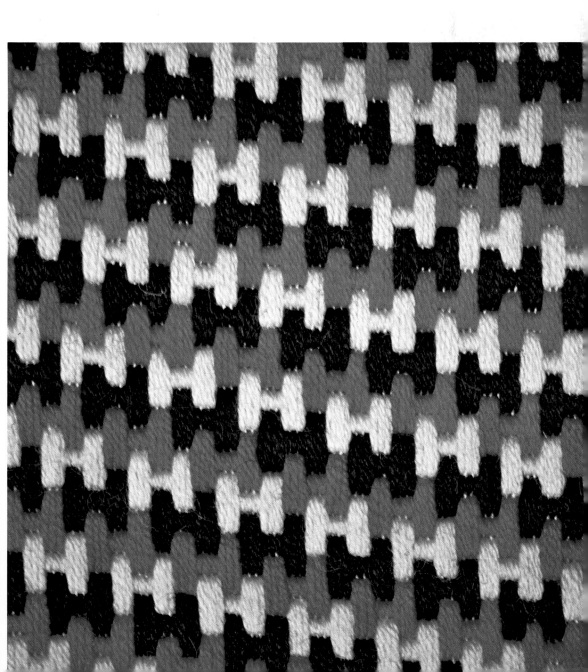

12

Fish Scales

This pattern is not far removed from Hungarian Ground. It is made up of three parallel "wavy" lines in three different colors worked over a 4-count. These rows surround offbeat oval shapes in a fourth color. All of the stitches in the oval scales are over a 4-count except the stitches one in from each side, which are over a 6-count. The accompanying diagram will help you set up the pattern, and the pattern is used in the Fish on pages 66–67.

You will notice that the upper and lower portions of the design have a very slight variation in count in the middle section. The difference is made up in the first wavy lines surrounding the middle. This kind of variation adds interest to a pattern.

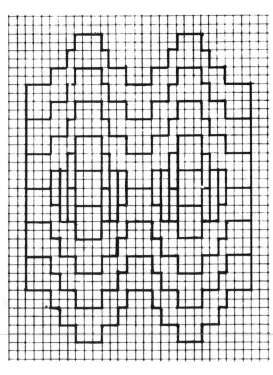

13

Shell Waves

Shell Waves is made up of broken and unbroken parallel rows of stitches. Nine colors have been used: three blues, three yellows, two greens, and black. Since the design is made up of short stitches, it is tight and durable. It would make an excellent covering for a bench or chair seat.

You can see how the design would change into a series of diamonds and circles if the broken scalloped row of dark blue were changed to black. Study the diagram and photograph carefully while setting up your canvas.

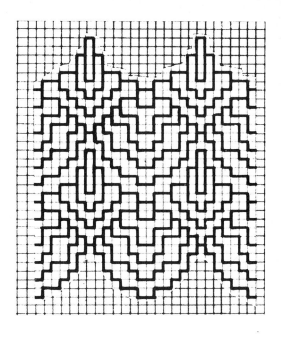

This design reproduced by permission of Ruth Heller, from Color and Stitch, *copyright 1971, Troubador Press, San Francisco, California, publisher.*

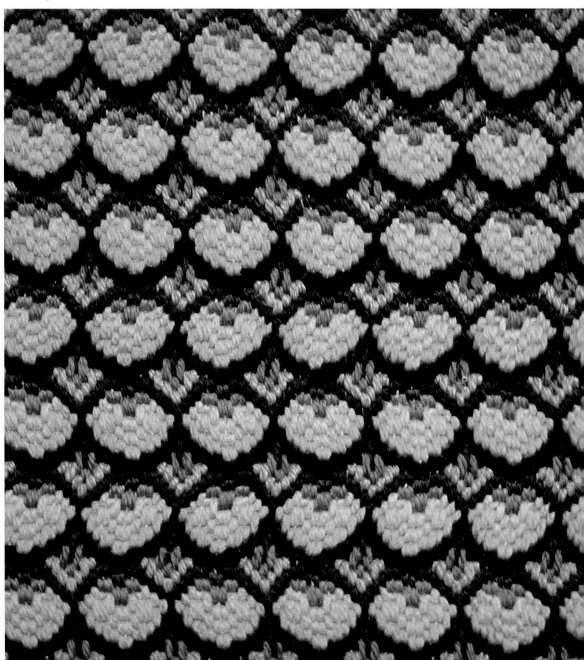

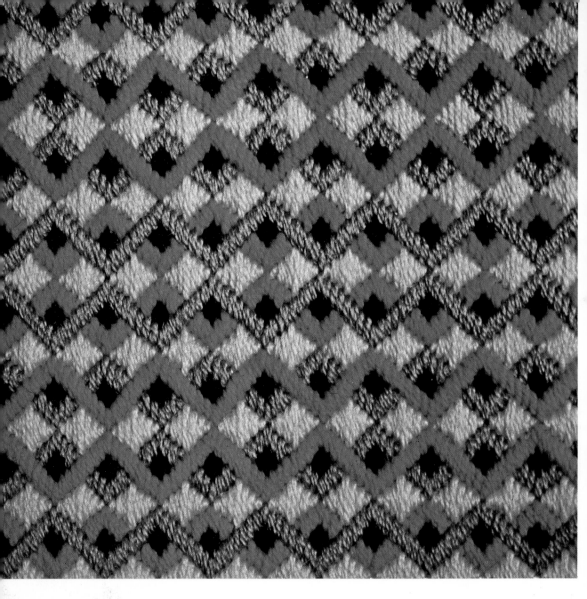

14

Rickrack

This pattern is worked in super-imposed zigzag rows with intervening large and small diamonds. The zigzag rows alternate in being "on top" or "underneath."

The easiest way to set up your canvas is to work an "on top" zigzag row over a 4-count advancing up or down one horizontal thread. Fill in an "underneath" zigzag next, and then work the diamonds. As a variation to the color scheme shown here, work all the "on top" zigzags in the first color and all the "underneath" zigzags in the second color.

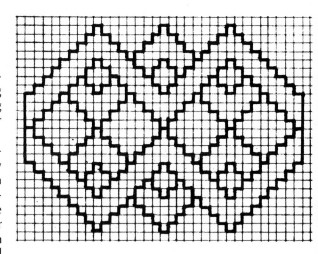

Mono canvas is generally more useful for Florentine embroidery than Penelope canvas. A good general mesh size for Florentine embroidery is thirteen or fourteen canvas threads to the inch.

15
Triangle Trees

This pattern is made up of regularly stacked interlocking triangles. The easiest way to set up the canvas is to work each group of triangles in vertical rows. If worked in two colors only, the upright trees should be dark and the upside down trees light. Use more colors to create perspective. This pattern is particularly well suited to pieces made in strips or for use as a border. You will note that when viewed sideways, the pattern looks like arrowheads.

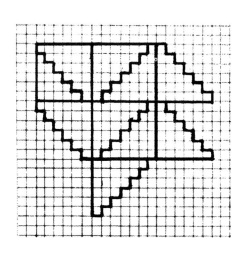

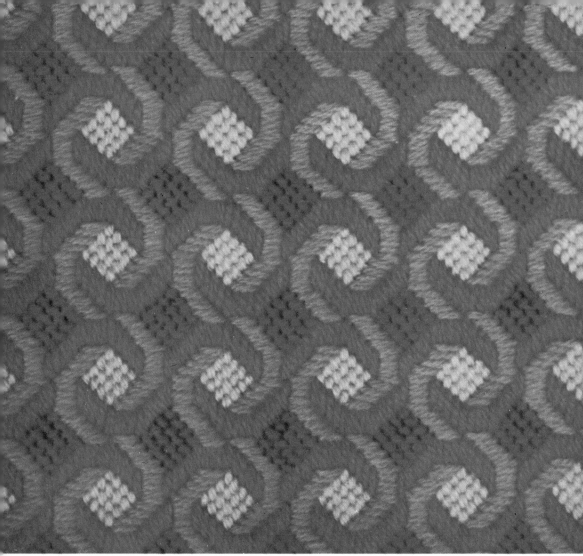

Original design by Mary Cooke Woodward, Washington, D.C.

Interlocked Chevrons

The symmetry and rhythm of this pattern will capture and hold your attention again and again. It is not only very pleasing to look at, but is one of the most fun to work on canvas. Set up opposing rows of chevrons (or "boomerangs") in the first color for a large section or the entire area to be covered. Count carefully! Then, work on the chevrons of the second color in the other direction.

Fill in the diamond spaces with 2-count Brick, or a large diamond unit as shown in Hungarian Ground, with the third and fourth colors, again alternating direction for added interest. This pattern is tight and enduring and would be excellent for projects that will receive hard wear.

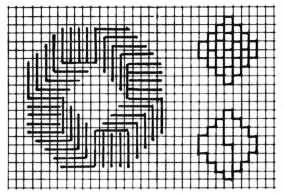

The chevrons cannot be graphed in block form since the stitches share holes. The lines here represent actual stitches, so this is a "duplication" of the pattern stitched on canvas.

Tweed

This stitch pattern looks like a "cheat" if the Bargello principle of not crossing canvas thread intersections is adhered to. Actually, an illusion of diagonal lines is created here in a pattern that is a great deal of fun to work up. Tweed is set up in two steps. Start the first color making pairs of vertical stitches over a 5-count, working in diagonal rows. Turn the canvas sideways and set up vertical pairs of stitches over a 5-count in the second color. You will notice after this step that there are little blocks of bare canvas showing through between the units of the first and second colors.

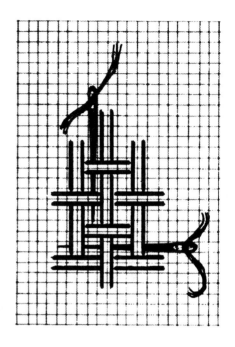

To fill in, secure a strand of the third color and bring it through to the surface of the canvas at the lower right corner. Weave it under the ends of the horizontal units, but stay on the *surface* of the canvas. Fill in all the rows and then turn the canvas sideways and start weaving again in the other direction, going under the ends of the horizontal units and over the first weaving threads.

When you are finished, it will appear that you have woven on the straight and the diagonal grains of the canvas to form a kind of latticework. This pattern works up very quickly and looks especially nice in a masculine setting, such as an office or den.

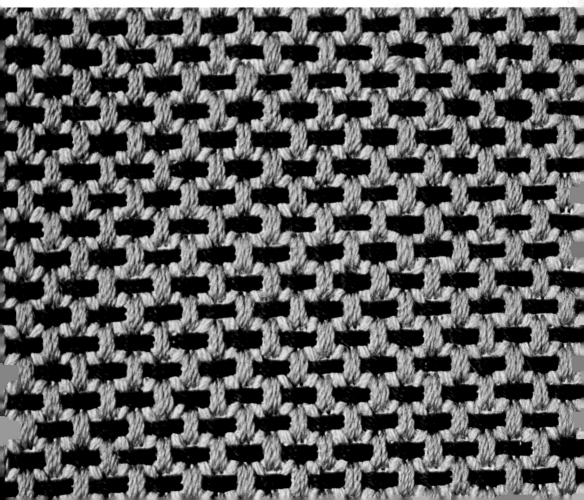

Laced Ribbons

This is another pattern based on units of Gobelin Droit. The "maze" is Gobelin Droit worked over a 6-count. The direction of stitching changes at regular intervals to form the mitered corners. This basic pattern could be expanded for a larger project by adding extra units. The "ribbons" laced through the maze are also a 6-count Gobelin Droit, and the background area has been done the same way (with a few small sections worked over a 3-count).

The use of Gobelin Droit has created a problem here, as you can see. Canvas shows through between the rows, detracting from the finished appearance of the design. Before this piece was mounted, backstitching in the background color was added to hide the canvas. It does this, and in addition, makes the embroidery more textured and interesting. Compare the black and white photograph with the color photograph of the evening purse to see the effect of the backstitching.

If you like this design but not the background, you could work the background in an interlocking stitch that will not create ridges, such as Brick or Parisian.

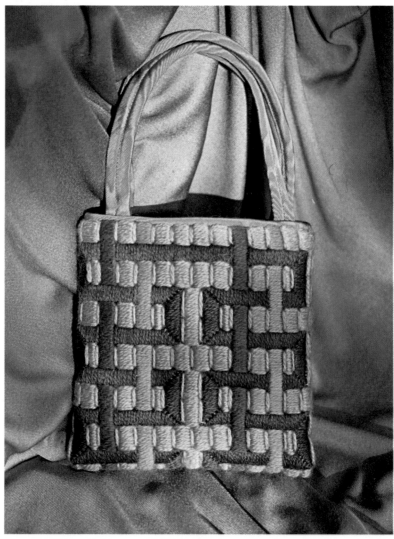

This little evening purse was made from the design shown in black and white on opposite page. Notice that lavender backstitching has been added to hide canvas that was showing through between the rows of Gobelin Droit. The piece was folded in half and mounted with pale green moiré silk. There is a small pocket inside to hold a compact or mirror.

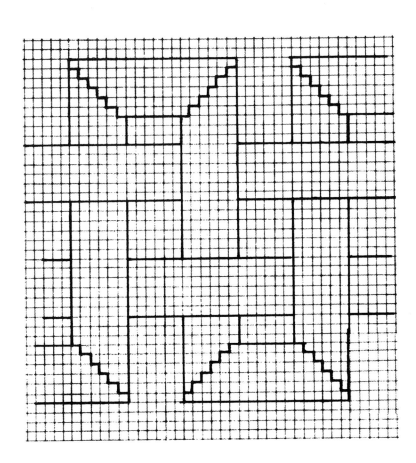

The Peasant Border design on page 40 has been used to make up this belt. After the piece was blocked, the edges were finished with the needlepoint binding stitch using black yarn. The excess canvas was trimmed and machine embroidered ribbon was hand-stitched to the back. This makes a very fancy lining; the belt is actually reversible. Wearing the belt inside out with the needlepoint as a lining is the ultimate snobbery!

New-Old Florentine Border Patterns

Certain Bargello patterns are particularly handsome when used in strips or in borders. Many items such as belts, luggage-rack straps, bookmarks, purse handles, and so on, are fine projects for Bargello stitchery. Also, mirror frames or picture frames and borders around other canvas work are places where Bargello can be used effectively.

The following four patterns were made for belts and will give you some ideas of how to approach designing a pattern for a long, narrow area. Sometimes you can take a section of a Bargello pattern, such as Triangle Trees on page 33, for use in this kind of shape. When working on a border or frame, keep in mind the scale of the center area and make sure you do not design a border that is overpowering or too skimpy for the central design theme.

Echo Border

The pattern is worked here so that the largest color areas touch at the outside. Quite a different effect could be produced by having contrasting colors touch along the edges. To widen the design, you might add stitches in the middle or change the single stitches to groupings throughout the pattern. The accompanying diagram will help you set the pattern up as it is shown here.

This design reproduced by permission of Ruth Heller, from Color and Stitch, *copyright 1971, Troubador Press, San Francisco, California, publisher.*

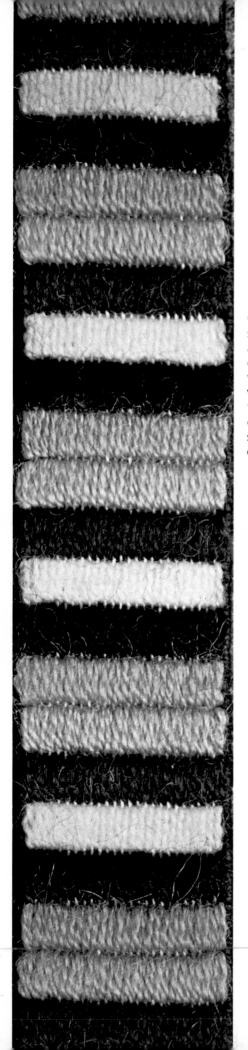

Ribbed Stripe Border

This is one of the most effective uses of Gobelin Droit you can make. Choose a color scheme to match several skirts and slacks or to accent colors in a room, and stitch parallel rows of Gobelin Droit. The rows can be as narrow or wide as you want, and they can be done over various counts. It is recommended, however, that you not use a stitch longer than an 8-count, or the finished piece will be susceptible to snagging. For variation, try working an uneven count "freehand" Gobelin.

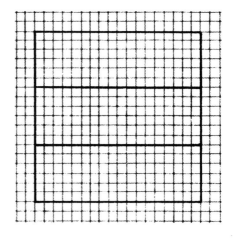

Tapestry yarn and Persian yarn are suitable for working Bargello. Persian yarn has three plies that separate; in some cases you may find it necessary to work with two plies instead of the full strand. Make a patch test of a new stitch to determine how well the yarn is going to cover the canvas.

21
Sawtooth Border

This pattern is another example of what can be done with the basic Bargello stitches to create a pleasing design. Old Florentine is worked here along the length of the piece outward from a central strip of Gobelin Droit. The piece could be made wider by adding more rows of Old Florentine.

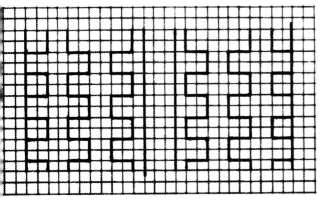

22
Peasant Border

This design was inspired by Indian bead-work patterns, which are an excellent source of ideas for contemporary Bargello. The diagram will help you get the design set up on canvas. Several rows of Peasant Border could be worked one below the other to cover a square project or could be alternated with other "strip" Bargello patterns to create the look of embroidered ribbons.

A color photograph of this design is shown on page 36.

This bright design shown on page 49 was made into a pincushion that is about 6" × 6" The backing fabric is green velvet. Pincushions make excellent baby gifts; an abstract Florentine pattern in gay colors is a pretty alternative to the "pink or blue" syndrome.

New Florentine Patterns

This section shows some new ways to use the Bargello filler stitches to create beautiful abstract designs. The following patterns may be ones that you will want to stitch as shown. However, they can also be used as a jumping-off point for your own design projects.

Do not make knots when beginning and ending strands of yarn. Weave a short tail of the yarn through the stitch backings on the reverse side of the canvas to secure it. Don't run dark colored thread under an area of light stitching, or the dark will show through.

This sampler could serve as the background for monograms or an alphabet worked in crewel stitches on top. Remember that it is perfectly suitable and often very attractive to mix different kinds of embroidery in the same piece.

23
Patchwork Sampler

Patchwork is the rage, and here is an opportunity for you to make a sampler of the Bargello filler stitches with very attractive end results. This is also an excellent way to use your leftover yarn.

Starting in the upper right, the stitches used are Tweed, and below that, a small section of Gobelin Droit and a section of Triangle Trees. On the bottom in the middle is a section of small-count Hungarian Ground and, to the left, Parisian in two colors. Above the Parisian is a traditional Bargello pattern found in the blanket of the Medieval Horse (on page 57). At the upper left is Zigzag in three colors, and in the middle is a Brick variation; stripes are created by working two colors in parallel diagonal rows. The stitches are over a 4-count with two in between each progression.

24

Symmetrical Tartan

You can create beautiful plaids using the Bargello filler stitches. In this one, a symmetrical section was taken from a larger plaid and blown up. The dark green corners are worked in Parisian, and the center red section is worked in a Brick variation over a 3-count (see diagram). The red-green sections are parallel diagonal rows of stitches over a 4-count with two canvas threads skipped at each step, and the white stripes are Gobelin Droit.

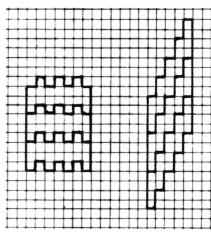

The Brick variation is on the left; the stripes are on the right.

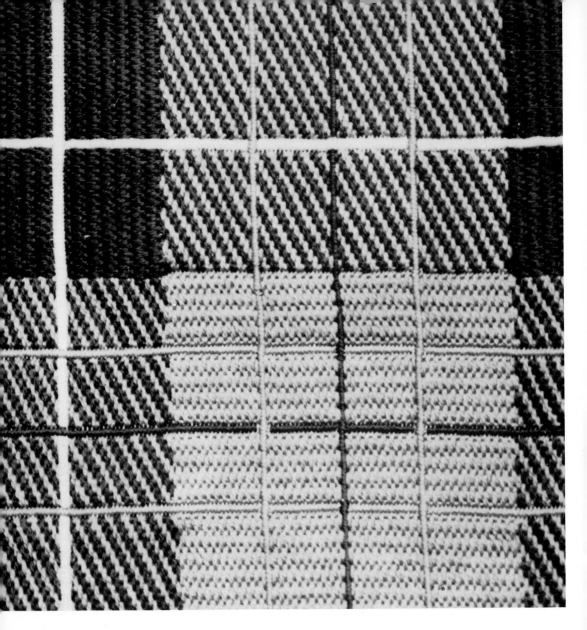

25

Asymmetrical Tartan

Here again, a small section of a tartan was taken and blown up to a larger size. This section is asymmetrical, which gives a lot of interest to the design. A Brick variation over a 4-count is used for the solid-color sections, while the stripes are created by parallel diagonal rows of stitches over a 4-count. The white and coral stripes that divide up the plaid are worked in Gobelin Droit.

Start each stitch from the bottom; pull the thread all the way through to the front of the canvas, and then in one motion end this stitch by poking the point of the needle to the back of the canvas and begin the next stitch by swinging the point of the needle to the next starting point. Pull the thread through to the surface again and repeat.

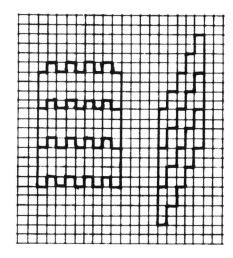

The Brick variation is on the left; the stripes are on the right.

A whole book could be made up of needlepoint tartans. The possible color combinations are virtually limitless, and the designs have a fresh, bold look that is pleasing to men and women alike. A tartan pillow makes a handsome personal gift and is fun to make. No drawing ability is necessary!

Oriental Medallion

The inspiration for this design came from a small motif in an oriental rug. Oriental rug books are a never-ending and excellent source of ideas for needlepoint and, in particular, contemporary Florentine work.

Oriental Medallion is the first of three designs in this book that have no top or bottom; they are symmetrical four ways and give the illusion of emanating from a kaleidoscope. There are directions in the section on design on how to set up four-way designs. They are especially appealing for the reason that the finished project is never upside down no matter what position it ends up in.

The diagram shows you how to set up one quarter of the design. The whole thing will fit together if you repeat what is shown three more times. Stitch the outline first and then fill in. The other diagram shows the center "flower" in full.

The outline is worked in Gobelin Droit (green). The stitches used to fill in are optional. You may want to substitute some of the stitches worked here for other favorites that you have. The white center background is 2-count Brick, and the center "flower" is mostly double 4-count Brick. The adjacent light blue section is Parisian, as are the copper-colored corner sections. The tan and navy squares on the four sides are double 4-count Brick; the white and navy squares at the corners are double 2-count Brick. The bittersweet sections are double 4-count Brick, and the white sections at the edges are basically 4-count Brick stitched to fit into the contour of the green outline. The light blue corners are done in parallel rows of 4-count stitches.

This diagram shows one quarter of the outline of the Oriental Medallion design. The stitch groupings are indicated. To make sure none of the design is "lost" when the piece is mounted, add an extra row of Gobelin Droit around the edges over a 2-count in colors matching adjacent areas.

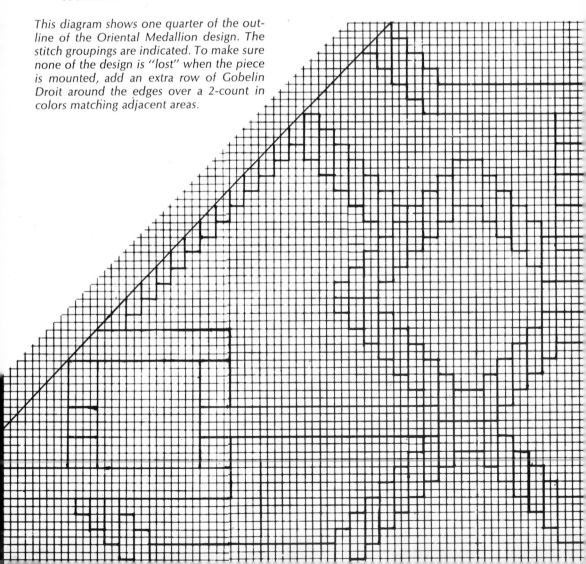

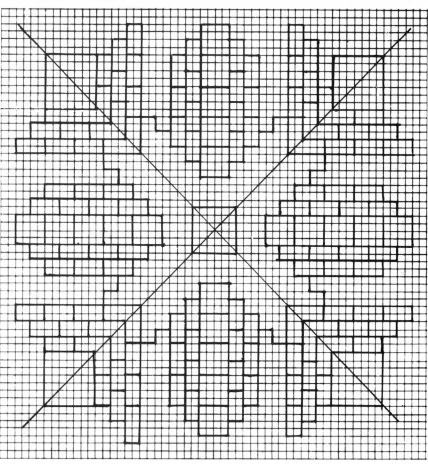

This diagram shows the center "flower" section in detail. The stitches along the seams, or diagonal lines, come together in the same holes.

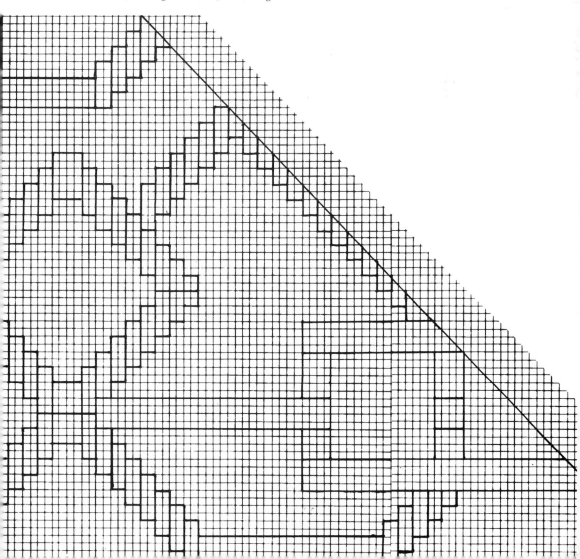

You will probably find it most comfortable to work from right to left on the canvas unless you are left-handed. In that case, try working from left to right.

27
Interlocked Frames

This is another design that is four-way and can be looked at from any angle. The design was worked out on graph paper first and then stitched on canvas. The essential stitch used is Gobelin Droit. The blue frame is worked on the true diagonal grain of the canvas; the stitches move up or down one canvas thread at each step. Notice how the corners miter together.

If you want to increase the size of this design, you can work in more interlocking frames at the outer edges. Make your revisions on graph paper before stitching.

Putting several of these squares together with different color combinations will create an afghan appearance.

This is an example of a pattern that cannot be diagrammed easily in "block" form. What is shown here is an actual facsimile of the stitches as worked on canvas. The basic count is over 7 canvas threads.

A color photograph of this design is shown on page 41.

28

Fantasy Trees

This magnificent design starts in the center with a flowerlike shape and emanates in four directions. You could stop the design at any point, depending on the size of the project you are making. In this case, the edges have been finished off with rows of Gobelin Droit, as you can see in the photograph of the stool.

This design calls for tight stitches, making the finished piece durable, snag-proof, and suitable for upholstery. Different design effects can be created by changing the color scheme. In the photograph here, you can see that the colors are reversed in alternate rows of trees, so there is light to dark in the greens and pinks, and then dark to light. You could make every other row of trees the same, with no reversing of shades. You might even want to stitch all five sections of each tree in the same color, making each row of trees a different color.

Another design option to consider is giving up the four-way property of the design and working rows of trees across a project without changing direction. In any case, to work the design as it is shown here, you must start from the center and work out.

This design reproduced by permission of Ruth Heller, from Color and Stitch, *copyright 1971, Troubador Press, San Francisco, California, publisher.*

Mrs. Heller's Fantasy Tree design was stitched in hot pinks and greens and used to recover an antique stool. The effect of the dark, warm wood with the contrasting "new"-looking colors is striking, and this piece of furniture would stand out in any room.

Using Florentine Stitches
in Representational Designs

The four designs that follow show how Bargello stitches can be used in pictorial, or representational, designs. The idea seems so natural and simple, it is amazing that this kind of use has not been put to the Florentine stitches in recent years. To find examples of Bargello "pictures," one must look in a museum.

You can really exercise your imagination when working out a design that calls for some Florentine stitches. You may want to use the filler stitches shown at the beginning of the book for certain sections, or you may want to invent a new stitch pattern to use in a section. Let the stitches you choose add their own statement of texture and movement to the design. The picture you are creating has a story to tell, but that is not the whole story. The stitches and colors will create the atmosphere.

You will notice in the animals that follow that there are areas that don't conform to an even, perfectly counted outline. The stitch patterns filling an area will have to be used in incomplete units in order to stay within the boundaries. These partial units may not exactly match the adjoining complete units, but you should try to blend them in as unobtrusively as possible.

You will also have to do some "freehand" stitching to make outlines and to fill in odd little shapes that are too small for a proper stitch-pattern unit. There aren't any rules for doing this. Experiment with the smallest, or tightest, stitches such as Gobelin Droit done with an even or uneven count, or with a 2-count Brick. Worry only about the finished appearance of the work. If you get to a point where you think an outline you are laboring over looks lumpy or jagged, put the piece down and step back from it a couple of feet. You will see that the lines smooth out when viewed at a slight distance.

These animals are shown here in black and white to demonstrate how much texture the Florentine stitch patterns can add to pictorial designs. These pieces are pleasing to view even in the absence of color. On the following pages, the animals appear in color with instructions for setting up the designs.

Medieval Horse

This stylized horse is made up of stitches shown at the beginning of the book. The horse's body is done in the large-count Hungarian Ground worked in contrasting colors. As you can see, this makes a very bold pattern, giving an extra decorative feeling to the space it fills in. The horse's mane and tail are worked in regular-count Hungarian Ground, and some details, such as the muzzle, are worked in Gobelin Droit.

The background is worked in Zigzag worked sideways to keep the larger stitch elements running in the same direction. (It was decided that the background would have interfered with the strong directional feeling of the stitches in the horse's body if the Zigzag stitch had been worked across the canvas.)

A detail of the pattern in the horse's blanket is shown here. This is a contemporary version of the traditional Bargello idea, and the stitch would make an attractive overall pattern for another project.

Above design reproduced by permission of Ruth Heller, from Color *and* Stitch, *copyright 1971, Troubador Press, San Francisco, California, publisher.*

Close-up of the horse-blanket pattern.

Rotate your canvas 180° at the ends of rows so that you will be working from right to left.

Medieval Horse

12"

14 x12

This diagram is really a sketch marked off on graph paper to show how the curves of a freehand drawing must be "stepped" to conform to the grid of needlepoint canvas. Depending on the stitch you use to fill a given pattern, the outline will shift slightly.

10 ½"

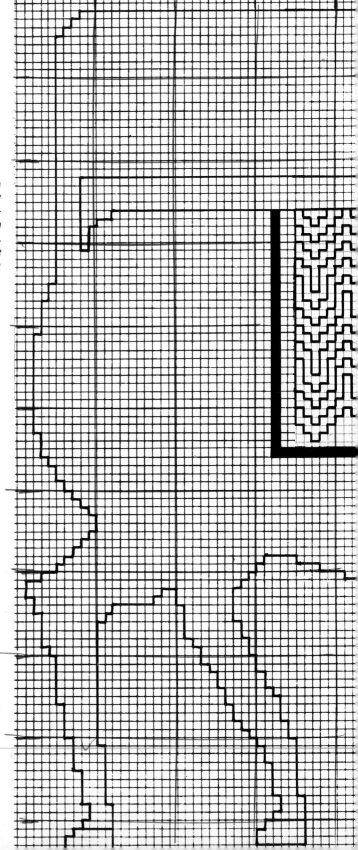

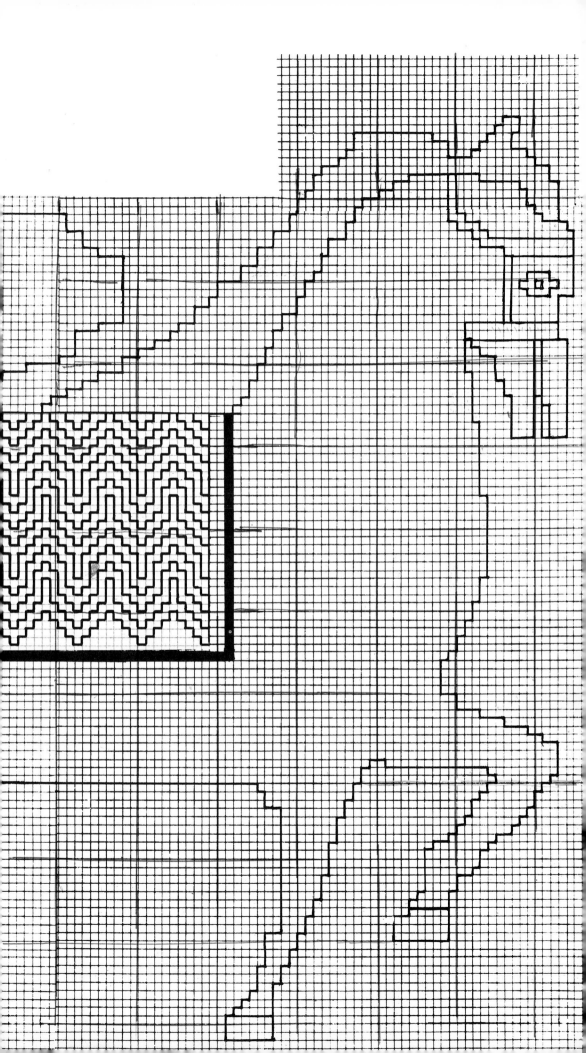

Circus Elephant

Ruth Heller's circus elephant definitely gives the impression that he is trotting along in a parade. It would look wonderful to use several elephants in a row with different colored blankets in a long, narrow project.

The elephant's body and ear are worked in double 4-count Brick, and the background is made up of parallel diagonal rows of stitches over a 4-count moving up or down one canvas thread with each stitch. A detail of the blanket pattern is shown here. Again, this pattern makes an attractive geometric repeat and would look very nice used by itself in another project.

You will notice that there are certain places that need outlining or defining, such as the trunk area and around the ear and headdress. You will have to work in uneven rows of stitches over a fairly small count to get the desired effect.

> When working with several shades of one color family, number the skeins to avoid confusion while stitching.

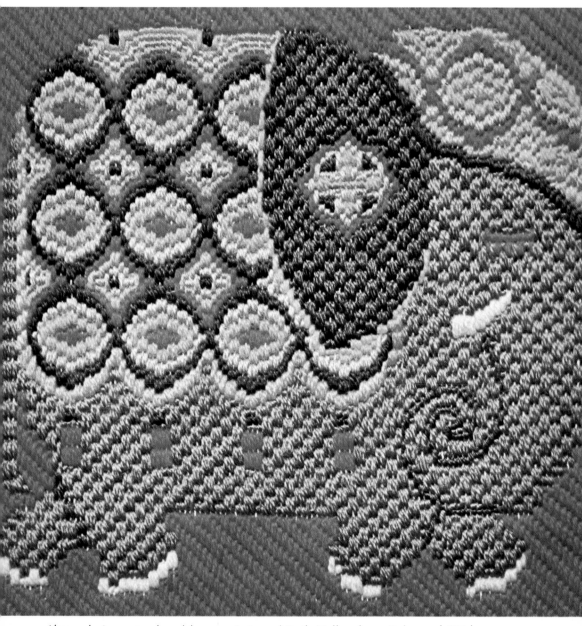

Above design reproduced by permission of Ruth Heller, from Color and Stitch, *copyright 1971, Troubador Press, San Francisco, California, publisher.*

Circus Elephant

Again, this outline is very useful in setting up the basic elephant design, but it may shift slightly depending on the stitch you use to fill in the elephant's body.

31
Rooster

Here is an example of how much interest is added to a design by the use of an outline stitched freehand according to the drawn design plan. The tail is first outlined in black and then filled in with Parisian, which is an excellent texture stitch. The rooster's comb and wattles are worked in single 2-count Brick, and the feet are in Gobelin Droit. The face, again, employs freehand stitching. The rooster's body is made up of a simple, but very effective repeat-diamond pattern, a detail of which is shown in the diagram. The background is double 2-count Brick, a stitch pattern that is reminiscent of barley.

The rooster's appeal is in his cascading tail, which forms a design within a design. Notice how a figure can be broken down into a series of interesting shapes that work together to form the whole. Of course, the balance of color is important in making this design come alive. Keep in mind the principle of sectioning space the next time you are working on a flower or piece of fruit, or whatever. Break up the figure into sections by the use of different colors or different stitches, or both.

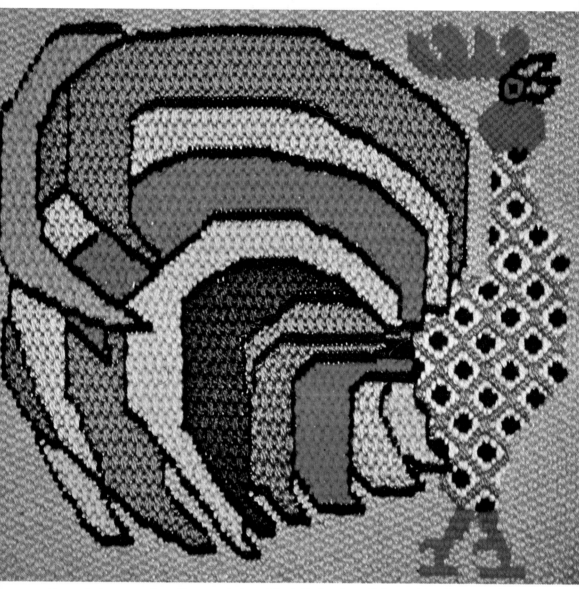

Above design reproduced by permission of Ruth Heller, from Color and Stitch, *copyright 1971, Troubador Press, San Francisco, California, publisher.*

Rooster

When working this design on canvas, it is easiest to outline the tail and then fill it in.

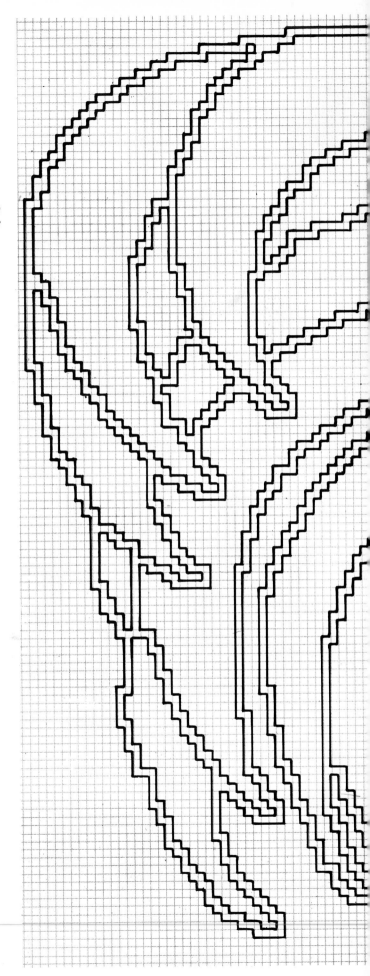

32 Fish

The inspiration for this fish came from a Chinese kite, which helps to account for the bright, fanciful colors. The stitches were chosen for this design because they give rhythm and movement to the swimming fish and surrounding water.

The background is a simplified version of Spools (stitch #9 on page 24). Here, a whole row is worked in one color instead of changing for each spool unit. Alternate rows are worked in very closely related tones of soft yellow. A ripply effect is created, giving interest to the background and making the fish look less "glued on."

The face is worked in double 2-count Brick, and the fins are made up of a simple diamond pattern shown here in the diagram. A Florentine Fish Scale pattern was concocted for the body. Freehand-stitched outlining done in black yarn was used to give emphasis to the design and to hide bare canvas. The finished piece is framed and *unglassed* so that the warmth of the yarn colors and the richness of texture show up immediately to the viewer.

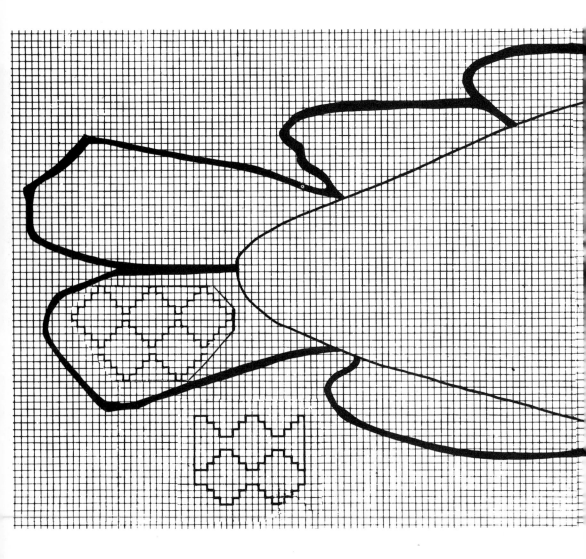

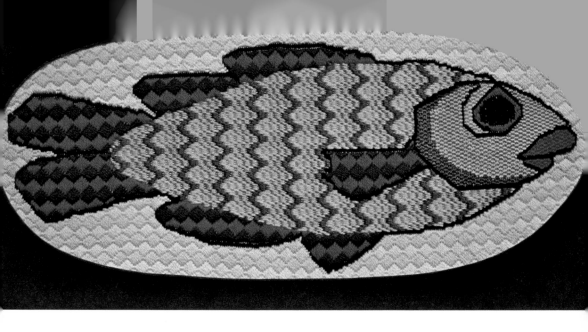

This "diagram" has been left in the natural curves of the original freehand drawing. As an exercise, take a pencil and a piece of tracing paper and convert the freehand drawing to a graphed design by stepping the lines to conform to the graph-paper grid.

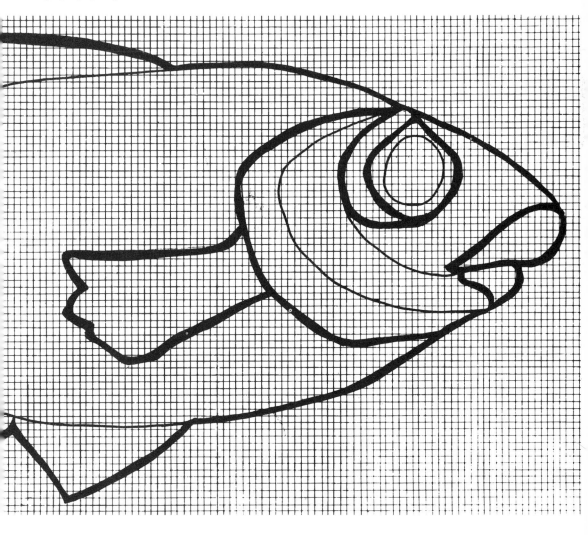

Notes on Design

Lots of people think they need to know how to draw (and draw well) in order to design their own needlepoint projects. Florentine work offers the perfect opportunity to sidestep the whole question of "artistic ability," since many of the designs are repeat geometrics and can be worked out with pencil and ruler on graph paper. And, for those who want to work on pictorial designs but are still worried about their talents, this author recommends investing in a pad of tracing paper!

The best way to plan shapes is to work them out on graph paper, which closely approximates the grid of the needlepoint canvas you will be using. There are different ways to approach graph-paper designing. First of all, you can pretend that the graph paper is actually the canvas; in other words, the lines of the paper are equivalent to the threads of the canvas. In this case, you will draw each individual stitch between lines exactly as it will fall on the canvas. This can be very helpful for working out "sticky" areas, but does not give you a very clear picture of how the total design will look when stitched up. Let it be said, however, that some designs (especially interlocking patterns with odd numbers of stitches) can be treated only in this manner on graph paper.

The other way to use graph paper is to think of the lines on the paper as *holes* on the canvas. In other words, the little squares would each represent a stitch location. It can be confusing to transpose a design blocked out in this manner onto canvas unless you remember that canvas threads "equal" graph-paper squares, and canvas holes "equal" graph-paper lines.

Some designs work out beautifully drawn out in this fashion, and you can get a good idea of the finished design, especially if you fill in the blocked off areas with the colors you intend to use. However, certain designs won't come out evenly if you try to graph them this way, and you will have to use the method of drawing on each stitch.

It will take a certain amount of experimentation in working out new designs, but the more experimenting you do, the more refined your ideas concerning the design at hand will become, and the more ideas you will generate for future designs.

These two pillows have the same design worked in reverse color combinations. The simple basket-weave design is set up in blocks of double 4-count Brick. A more complex basket weave can be created by using two colors in each direction instead of one. Designs like this are easy to work out on graph paper and have a great decorative look.

Use very dark colors in small areas or thin lines only, since the stitch definition is lost, and no texture will show through.

This pattern is a slightly more involved version of Shaded Peaks, which is shown on page 23. In this pattern, zigzag lines are added between the tallest peaks. The design was worked on graph paper and stitched on canvas in identical parallel rows. This design is shown with the Oriental Medallion pillow in the frontispiece on page 6.

Planning shapes, of course, is only half of your work. Color must be considered along with shape, or line, in creating new designs. You may want to use colored pencils on tracing paper over your graphed design until you reach a pleasing combination. Then, to get a true picture, you should work with the yarns themselves, putting together different combinations before making your final decision.

Sometimes, even after you are "sure" of a color scheme, the colors will change their appearance after they are stitched up, and you may have to modify as you work. One advantage to Florentine work is that it is not necessary to paint the underlying canvas, and therefore color changes can be made midstream without affecting the finished look of the project except for the better.

Once you have settled on the design shapes and colors, it is helpful to stitch a section to make doubly sure that the stitch count is correct and that the colors work the way you want them to. This patch test will also indicate whether the yarn is covering the canvas adequately. Occasionally, you may misread your graph drawing, or you may think some pattern will work on canvas because it works on paper. Stitching a sample may sound like a lot of extra effort, but the end results will show your care and planning.

The actual process of stitching your design into a finished piece of embroidery is one of the most satisfying aspects of the project, and you may be sad to see the last stitch fall into place (like coming to the end of a good book), even though you're ready to move along to the next artistic endeavor. As you go along, always remember to stand back from your work occasionally, and invite the comments of your family and friends. This critiquing will improve your work and add to the fun of your Bargello needlepoint experience.

This owl chair, made by the author for her young nephew, combines Bargello with other needlepoint stitches. The owl's wings are in a simple scallop pattern made to resemble feathers, and the background is worked in large-count Hungarian Ground.

To enlarge or reduce a design you want to use, have a positive photostat made to the desired dimensions and then graph the design on paper with squares per inch equivalent to the project canvas size.

or

A graphed pattern can be enlarged or reduced by regraphing on another gauge paper (more or fewer blocks per inch).

Patti Rogers of Houston settled on a simple Florentine design for this tennis racquet cover made for her father. The zigzags surround a strip of Diagonal Tent in which a monogram is worked. The highly contrasting, bright colors add to the boldness of the design.

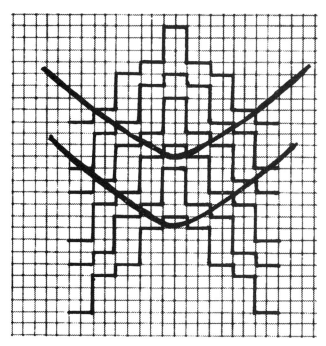

Most of the designs shown in this book that follow traditional Florentine "rules" use parallel rows of stitches that are identical. Very attractive designs can be created by varying this basic formula to include alternate rows of different length stitches. This diagram shows a simple design composed of rows that follow a 4-2-4-2-4 count, and then in the subsequent row, a 2-4-2-4-2 count. An interesting thing happens within the design. The strong directional feeling of the rows is maintained, of course, through color. But another element is added; scallops or garlands appear to be formed from the similar-count stitching groups that are located next to each other. This is indicated by the curved lines. Try alternating, or reversing, the count in subsequent rows in one of your designs for an interesting change.

This pillow, worked by Mrs. William S. Manuel III of Houston, has a very bold look due to the highly contrasting colors and the strong scalloped design. Every other row reverses the stitch length, or count, which adds a new dimension to the pattern.

The kaleidoscopic, or four-way, Bargello patterns have become extremely popular to work. There are a few tricks to setting up these designs that may save you hours of ripping out once you begin to stitch. Let your inspiration come from cut-paper designs. Experiment by cutting squares of paper folded in half and then in half again; you should have a stack of four small squares now. Fold in half once more to form a triangle and cut an outline and various "internal" sections. Unfold and see what you have. Keep working on cutouts until you get a design you want to stitch.

The first step is to transfer your cut, or freehand, design to graph paper. Mark vertical and horizontal intersecting lines in the center of the paper, and then mark the true bias diagonal lines through the central intersection. The diagonal lines will cut each quadrant in half. The direction of stitching changes at the bias, or diagonal, seams, and you should keep this in mind when deciding how to orient your design on the graph paper.

Lay your cutout design on the graph paper, matching midline and diagonal folds with midline and diagonal lines, and trace around the main sections. The next thing you must do is convert the curves and slanted lines of the original tracing to conform to the grid of the graph paper. Make sure that each quadrant matches the rest and that each half of a quadrant is a "reverse carbon."

There is no set rule for laying out the parallel rows of stitches that fill in the body of the design. Some people start from the middle and work out, using pencil so they can erase. Other people work from the outline in toward the center. One thing to keep in mind in "stepping out" the rows is

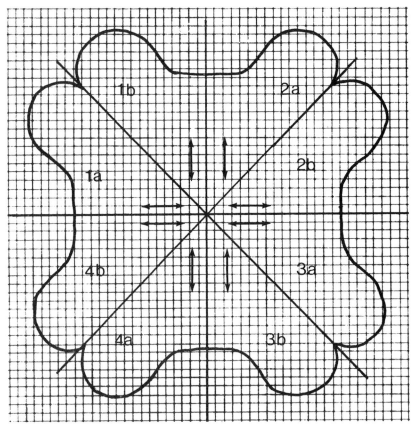

To set up a four-way Bargello design, intersecting lines must first be drawn to divide the canvas equally into quadrants. The seams, or mitered lines, will fall along the diagonal lines; it is here that the stitching changes direction. The two halves of each quadrant will form mirror images, and quadrants 1, 2, 3, and 4 are identical. The outline in this diagram was made by cutting a square of folded paper and tracing onto graph paper.

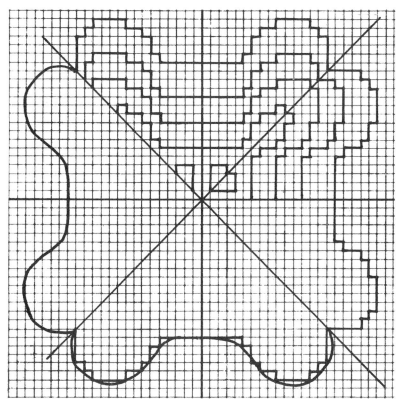

This diagram shows the development of the design from a simple outline. First the curves of the original drawing must be stepped to conform to the grid of the graph paper. Then rows of stitches are set up which are parallel to the outline. Stitches meeting at the diagonal seams enter the same hole.

that very long stitches (worked over eight or more canvas threads) will be susceptible to snagging and will limit the use given to the finished piece. Therefore, try to set up rows or areas of stitches over fewer than eight threads. To get a really accurate idea of what the final design will look like, color in the various rows with the color shades you are planning to use.

Now you are ready to start on the canvas. Mark off intersecting vertical and horizontal midlines with pencil (the pencil will follow the groove between threads—do not try to draw on top of them), and then draw the diagonals. You will notice that all these lines cross through one hole in the very center of the canvas. This is "home base."

Look at your graphed design again. Chances are there are an *even* number of stitches (two, four, or six) going into "home base," and this works just fine on paper. But, if you work with an even number of stitches on canvas, the design will be thrown off to the side by one stitch, so you will have to add or subtract a stitch from the design in order to have an *odd* number coming into home base. This compensation is necessary only at the vertical and horizontal midlines. Don't let it throw you, and don't bother to try changing your graphed drawing. Just add or subtract when you start stitching.

There is less chance of making a counting error if you work from the middle out toward the edges of the design, but this is not necessary, and you may find it more interesting to "hop" around. Just make sure that everything is mirror-imaged at the diagonal seams. If you have large sections that need filling in, remember the stitches shown at the beginning of the book. Any of these stitches would also be suitable to use around the outside of your four-way creation.

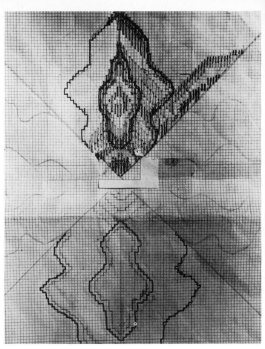

A very simple cut-paper design by Sally Boom of Houston was sketched on graph paper and further experimented with and refined at this stage. Mrs. Boom decided to orient the large shapes along the vertical and horizontal midlines of the canvas; however, these shapes could also have been placed on the diagonal seams. Her stitched piece, shown here in process, is worked in shades of soft moss greens.

Lillian Shetler of Houston developed a very bold, geometric design in bright oranges and greens from her cut-paper pattern. Notice how she has used 2-count Brick in the center of the design and Parisian around the central box shape. A Gobelin Droit border finishes the piece off nicely.

This four-way piece, worked in pinks and greens, could be entitled "Vibrations." It was developed from a cut-paper pattern and worked by Mary Nall of Houston.

Jeane Aston of Houston used shades of gold to deep brown for her four-way Bargello piece, inspired by a cut-paper pattern. She has used the traditional Tent stitch to surround the central design and has added a Gobelin Droit border to the edges.

In these pillows, many sections of four-way stitching are put together to form box patterns. The design possibilities based on the idea of boxes are endless. As you can see, the stitching is done in both directions, with box edges meeting at the diagonal seams. The actual stitches are over a 6-count with one canvas thread at each step, except in the smallest squares, which have a 1-3-5-7-5-3-1-count, and where the ends of rows must taper down at the mitering points. Here, the stitches decrease to 5, then 3, then 1 right at the seam lines. Worked by Mrs. William S. Manuel III of Houston.

Index

Numbers in parentheses ( ) indicate stitch pattern numbers.

A

Asymmetrical Tartan (25), 44, 45

B

Bargello
    four-way patterns, 74–78
    history of, 7–13
beginning and ending threads (Hint), 41
belt, 36
Brick (1), 15

C

canvas margin allowance (Hint), 20
canvas types and sizes (Hint), 30
centering the design, 22
changing stitch length in alternating
    rows, 73
Circus Elephant (30), 53, 58–61
    full-size diagram, 60–61
color, 70
colorfast project materials (Hint), 25
correcting errors (Hint), 71

D

designing with graph paper, 68
direction of working (Hint), 48

E

Echo Border (19), 37
enlarging and reducing designs:
    graph paper, photostats (Hint), 72
evening purse, 34, 35

F

Fantasy Trees (28), 50–51
Fish (32), 66–67
Fish Scales (12), 28, 66–67
flame stitch, 7
Florentine Embroidery, 7

Florentine Filler Stitches, 14–21
    Brick (1), 15
    Gobelin Droit (2), 16
    Hungarian (3), 17
    Hungarian Ground (4), 18
    Old Florentine (6), 20
    Parisian (5), 19
    Zigzag (7), 12, 21
four-way Bargello patterns, 74–78
    "box" pattern variations, 78
    designing from paper cutouts, 74
    filling in the design outlines, 74–75
    original designs from paper cutouts,
        76, 77, 78
    transferring designs to graph paper,
        74
    working out the design on canvas, 75

G

Goal Posts (11), 27
Gobelin Droit (2), 16
graph paper designing, 68
graphed designs,
    "basket-weave" pillows, 69
    "peaks and valleys" pillow, 6, 70

H

Hints
    beginning and ending threads, 41
    canvas margin allowance, 20
    canvas types and sizes, 30
    colorfast project materials, 25
    correcting errors, 71
    direction of working, 48
    enlarging and reducing designs, 72
    how to stitch, 45
    keeping the project clean, 63
    protecting canvas edges, 14
    rotating the canvas, 55
    stitching rows for seam, 20
    use of dark colors, 69
    working with several shades, 58
    yarn types and thickness, 38
how to stitch (Hint), 45

Hungarian (3), 17
Hungarian Ground (4), 18
Hungarian Point, 7

I

Interlocked Chevrons (16), 32
Interlocked Frames, 41, 49

K

Kaleidoscope Bargello patterns, 74–78
    See also four-way Bargello
Keeping the project clean (Hint), 63

L

Laced Ribbons (18), 34–35

M

Medieval Horse (29), 52, 54–57
    full-size diagram, 56–57
    horse blanket detail, 55

N

New Florentine Patterns, 41–51
    Asymmetrical Tartan (25), 44, 45
    Fantasy Trees (28), 50–51
    Interlocked Frames (27), 49
    Oriental Medallion (26), 6, 46–48
    Patchwork Sampler (23), 42
    Symmetrical Tartan (24), 43, 45
New-Old Florentine Patterns, 22–35
    Fish Scales (12), 28
    Goal Posts (11), 27
    Interlocked Chevrons (16) (Cover), 32
    Laced Ribbons (18), 34–35
    Op Boxes (10), 26
    Rickrack (14), 22, 30
    Shaded Peaks (8), 23
    Shell Waves (13), 29
    Spools (9), 24–25
    Triangle Trees (15), 31
    Tweed (17), 33
New-Old Florentine Border Patterns,
    36–40
    Echo Border (19), 37
    Peasant Border (22), 36, 40
    Ribbed Stripe Border (20), 38
    Sawtooth Border (21), 39
Notes on Design, 68–78

O

Old Florentine (6), 20
Op Boxes (10), 26
Oriental Medallion (26), 6, 46–48
    diagrams, 46–47

owl chair, 71

P

Parisian (5), 19
Patchwork Sampler (23), 42
peaked Florentine design (pillow), 6, 70
Peasant Border (22), 36, 40

R

reducing and enlarging designs
    graph paper, photostats (Hint), 72
Ribbed Stripe Border (20), 38
Rickrack, 22, 30
Rooster, 53, 62–65
rotating the canvas (Hint), 55
ruffled pillow, 25

S

Sawtooth Border (21), 39
scallop pattern pillow, 73
Shaded Peaks (8), 23
Shell Waves (13), 29
Spools (9), 24–25
stitching rows for seam (Hint), 20
stool, 51
Symmetrical Tartan (24), 43, 45

T

tennis racquet cover, 72
tracing paper, 70
Triangle Trees (15), 31
Tweed (17), 33

U

use of dark colors (Hint), 69
Using Florentine Stitches in
    Circus Elephant (30), 53, 58–61
    Fish (32), 66–67
    Medieval Horse (29), 52, 54–57
    Representational Designs, 52–67
    Rooster (31), 53, 62–65

W

working with several shades (Hint), 58

Y

yarn coverage patch-test, 70
yarn types and thickness (Hint), 38

Z

Zigzag, 12, 21